Enduring Words

A Collection of Creative Work by Prisoners

Edited by
Arkbound Foundation

Enduring Words:
A Collection of Creative Work by Prisoners

Edited by Arkbound Foundation

© Arkbound Foundation

ISBN: 9781912092987

First published in 2023 by Arkbound (Publishers)

Cover image by Tasmin Briers

No part of this publication may be reproduced, stored in a retrieval system, or transmitted, in any form or by any means without the prior permission of the publisher, nor be otherwise circulated in any form of binding or cover other than that in which it is published and without a similar condition being imposed on the subsequent purchaser.

Arkbound is a social enterprise that aims to promote social inclusion, community development and artistic talent. It sponsors publications by disadvantaged authors and covers issues that engage wider social concerns. Arkbound fully embraces sustainability and environmental protection. It endeavours to use material that is renewable, recyclable or sourced from sustainable forest.

Arkbound
4 Rogart Street Campus
Glasgow
G40 2AA

www.arkbound.com

Enduring Words

A Collection of Creative Work by Prisoners

Editor's Note

This collection of creative work arose from a National Writing Competition in 2022 ('Writing Within Walls') that was open to people with experience of being in custody or on probation. The chosen theme of the competition was 'Endurance'. After receiving over 100 eligible entries, three judges then had the challenging task of selecting 20 winning entrants. The book showcases these, though the total number of separate pieces featured are 23.

To find out more about the Writing Within Walls project, please visit **www.arkfound.org.uk** or write to us at Arkbound Foundation, 4 Rogart Street, Glasgow G40 2AA.

Foreword:
Unleashing the Power of Creative Writing Behind Bars

Creative writing, with its capacity to ignite imagination, articulate emotions, and foster personal growth, emerges as a beacon of hope within the criminal justice system. It always amazes me when I see the talent that exists in prison settings and how the power of language and stories can flourish. Whether through poetry, lyrics or full fiction writing, people draw from their emotions, memories, and dreams.

In the act of writing, people reclaim their agency, forge a connection to their inner selves, and embark on a journey of self-discovery and personal reflection. It's also an enjoyable, constructive way to use time, something that prisoners have in abundance.

Creative writing nurtures a myriad of essential skills and through their engagement with writing individuals refine their literacy and communication abilities and enhance their fluency, vocabulary, and critical thinking. The process of crafting words into sentences, and sentences into stories, empowers writers to explore their inner worlds with clarity and depth. It provides them with the tools to articulate their experiences, transcend their circumstances, and give voice to the often-unheard stories that dwell within prison walls.

Moreover, creative writing opportunities create a sense of community and connectivity. A space for collaboration, within which some people find solidarity, and often such writing opportunities serve as a powerful reminder that individuals are more than their mistakes — they are storytellers, creators, and agents of change.

This collection of writings, from incarcerated individuals, offers a glimpse into the transformative power of creative writing in prison. Within these pages, the stories, poems, and reflections transport us to the depths of human experiences, bridging the gap between confinement and freedom. These voices demand to be heard, reminding us of the resilience and potential for growth that reside within each person, regardless of their past.

Common themes in the writings include reflection, finding strength within themselves, developing resilience and a sense of empowerment despite their circumstances and I enjoyed reading the learners thoughts and understanding how getting them down on paper forms part of their rehabilitation process.

Judging the entries was a difficult, time-consuming task and 'what' makes a good piece of creative writing is something I found myself considering. Each entry had its own merit, as it captured an individual's own take on the theme and the fact that people had put pen to paper and even considered engaging deserves credit. As I read through the entries, I found that originality and the writers authentic voice captured my attention most of all, it engaged my imagination and immersed me in their narrative, so it was these entries that I collated in my pile to consider with the other judges.

I have worked in prison education for 17 years and over that time I have seen the power that creative opportunities can have on individuals. They provide platforms to engage and empower, as well as a means of supporting wellbeing. It is through these new opportunities that people can develop new skills, form new identities, and ultimately make changes to their lives.

Sarah Hartley
Lancashire, 2023

Sarah Hartley is National Lead for Creative Strategies at NOVUS, Co-Chair of the National Criminal Justice Alliance, active mentor, and has been involved in prison education for 17 years.

First Impression
Syed Langstaff-Hayes

The first time I saw him, punching away at keys on a computer, I barely noticed him. He wasn't spectacular or good-looking in the traditional sense, not the usual jack-the-lad, boasting with needless pseudo-confidence. Being honest, I don't think he noticed me either. He was searching feverishly through pages of scrawled notes, some strange long-forgotten language to me or you, but which appeared to make sense to him.

When we were introduced, he gave a sheepish smile, mumbling some sort of greeting. Little did I know this person was about to change my life. I had met one of the most inspiring, strong-willed people that ever walked the earth. There was no cosmic click, the one we see in movies, where strangers bump into each other and fall in love. For us, I don't know exactly when that click happened, but in that first moment, I didn't think we would speak again.

Maybe that would have been for the best. Things would have been much simpler. I'm not saying I regret what happened, quite the opposite actually. He really did change my life. My view of the world became less cynical. I saw potential around me. Maybe I was projecting my feelings onto other things, but I suppose it doesn't matter. The important thing was I felt hopeful for the first time in what seemed a lifetime. A flame burst to life inside me, like a solar flare radiating outwards, spreading warmth, energy and nourishment throughout my very soul.

Fire, though, is a tricky thing, craving fuel, and it eventually becomes all-consuming. Every waking moment, I wanted to spend with him. It was almost an addiction. I wanted to... no... needed to impress him. This was new; I'd never felt so insecure and needed validation. This approval did not come freely, or maybe it did and I couldn't see it through the smoke. Trying to read him was like deciphering the cryptic hieroglyphs he was working on the first time we met. I was suspended in time, lost in his brown eyes. I wouldn't have cared if the world ended right then and there. I would die a happy man.

'What?' he used to say with a playful smile, suggesting he already knew the answer. He wanted me to say it.

'Nothing,' I said. Always nothing. Maybe it wasn't him that was afraid to offer validation after all. I knew exactly what I wanted to say. I'm sure you can guess. No matter, those words would not come out.

Isn't it strange how one 'insignificant' moment can change the trajectory of your life, shredding plans and dreams into confetti? I'm not one to believe in fate or destiny, because if they exist they're sadistic sickos. They don't lay down plans that lead towards our happily-ever-after. No. They tease us, showing what we could have. They torment us, keeping it just out of reach. They torture us, covering the pathway with pain.

Falling in love in prison is far from ideal. You'd think being stuck in a confined area would make it easier. Think again. The fleeting, stolen moments serve to heighten the sense of loneliness. The fear of being caught ruining the moment. Caught – as if this primal emotion was a crime. It's not that long ago it was a crime. I often wondered if some man, long forgotten to anyone who now roams these wings, once sat where I do today simply because he was gay. I guess we haven't progressed that much.

We did, however, make the most of it. Brief moments imprisoned me in a different type of cage. One that wasn't as desolate as the one I was physically in but one that made me equally as powerless. The graffiti on the walls told a story of dreams and future plans. The bed was warm and welcoming, just like his arms. Escapism of the highest calibre. Checking back into reality was all the more difficult. The whole point of prison is to prevent you from escaping. I suppose it is doing its job.

Prison life is bleak, for the most part devoid of physical contact or emotion from the nurturing end of the spectrum. Personally, when I found even a shred of it after such a long time, I was gripped by the intensity, overwhelmed and, at times, I thought it would suffocate me. We all have a safe space we go to when things get too much, a place in our mind full of rainbows and unicorns. Even my safe space was causing me anxiety.

As the months drew on, I retreated into myself, or more accurately further away from him. I hated myself because of this. It wasn't necessarily a choice, it was the reflex that makes you pull your hand away from fire. I was protecting myself, and him. In those moments, I could see I was sabotaging myself, as a punishment. I didn't deserve to be happy. There was no happily-ever-after in my story, only the sinister fairy-tale ending.

In the end I had to make a decision, one of the hardest decisions ever. Did I make the right one? Who knows? Was the choice even mine to make? You had better ask fate! Maybe it would've been better if we'd never spoken again, but I regret nothing because, as a result of that seemingly mundane moment, I had the strength to stand up tall against the weight of an institution that was trying day and night to crush me. I learned I wasn't alone; we don't have to look deep within ourselves to find courage, rather we need to look outwards and take strength from our connections with other people. One man does not make an army to fight the war that is life. We need fire to stay warm, but it also makes a good weapon if we take time to understand how to care for it. When we are loved, and we allow ourselves to be loved, we are indestructible.

My Land, My Home
Ekimlláh

I still live bound to you, the memories enslaved by my thoughts; shackled to you, I thrive on your colours of green, black and yellow. The beauty of your landscape is adorned with the abundance of trees, the Blue Mountain peaks and the many rivers that flow across the land as far as the eye can see. You are known as the land of wood and water. It is easy to see why.

I breathe the redolence released as the rain soaks the rich fertile soil made hard by the beating Caribbean sun. Now the rainwaters are flowing, flooding and renewing the land. For so many years I have missed your smile, the humility of your people, their spirits never broken, always colourful in their attire, language and culture, constantly revelling in the pulsating beat of reggae music.

The Rio Grande always flows from the surrounding mountain range. Bamboo rafts will leave the river banks from sunrise to sundown, loaded with those who arrive in their thousands. They come to soak up the natural tranquil beauty of the never-ending landscape, while sipping on the sugar cane rum, infused with juices of the tropical fruits indigenous to the island. How I miss this familiarity.

I can still see the curling smoke rising from the jerk pits as it makes its way up into the ever-blue sunlit skies. The aroma of the pan cooked meats, the mouth-watering fried fish, coupled with the sweet doughy bread as a side dish. Curried goat, ox-tail, stew peas and rice. How I crave these dinner delicacies. Lunch: I often dined on the exquisiteness of patties and meatloaves with various fillings; a sugar bun or a sandwich of cornbread and cheese, normally washed down with a cool juice box of infinite variety. How I miss crunching the sugar cane sticks and expelling the fibres once they are rendered bone dry. Mangoes with the smell of the tropical rain, the stickiness of jackfruit, the tanginess of the sun-ripe oranges, the sweetness of the ever bearing, irresistible naseberries and the crunchiness of refreshing watermelons. All gifts from Mother Earth, which belong, not just to a chosen few, but for all to share.

The old life continues, only the colours of the heavens will change. I will never fall prey to mental or physical depravity but remain beholden for what I have achieved and forfeited. Displaced, I have been; but I will never be disconnected or depart from you. I stand against those who dare to take or dilute my love for you and those that endeavour to steal the thoughts from the sanctuary of my mind.

My memories can and never will be erased as they are indelibly marked in my mind. I will be forever grateful that you are always close to my heart. I will never be led away from you, neither will I be turned around or interrupted by intimidation because I know my inaction and inertia will be the inheritance of the next generation. I reminisce through lost time for myself, my soul, the nucleus of my existence which brings me full circle, right back to you, safe in your arms where I belong. I dedicate myself to you, my spirit dissolves within you, a blazing happiness engulfs me, and joy overwhelms me when I am with you. There is this burning desire to return home to Jamaica, the land of my birth, my beginning, my roots, where I will enjoy the rest of my days till my soul is laid to rest.

Prison Priorities

Piaras Heatley

In the beginning…. I saw the wasted potential around me…
In the beginning I saw how people are misjudged…..

      ……I used to be on the outside

looking in, and never saw myself as part of this ugly machine…
churning out personality disorders, and complexes….

Now I am the wasted potential…

      …Now I am the waste in the wind…

The wild wood, tree

    falls

      slowly,

        but not without grace….

I have arrived at this destination….

      …..and the hole in
the ground that I have shattered shows my resolute silence,

and only when I have achieved what I set out for...

                                        ....only then will I rest..

Now I am part of this machine,

Now I am the wasted potential,

Now I am the excuse from a broken system....

                                        ....I will be
the spanner in the works, and I will use these tools to mend the broken home in which we all live...

Why I Read

Phil P.

I read for the pleasure, an escape from this place,
To far away galaxies, beyond time and space,
A remote rum-kissed island, to mountain peaks covered in snow,
To the depths of the ocean, to cold arctic slopes.

I read for the humour, an escape from this cell,
Comics with their stories and the jokes that they tell.
If I'm struggling with lockdown, been down for a while,
I get lost in a story and pretty soon I can smile.

I read for the horror, an escape over this fence,
A grisly whodunnit that maintains the suspense,
Or a gripping conundrum, the pages eager to turn,
The culprit unmasked, their identity, I can't wait to learn.

I read for the bravery, an escape from this wing,
Of valour and service before queen or the king,
Heroes without capes and the sacrifice they gave,
Extraordinary discoveries, how many lives have they saved?

I read for the knowledge, an escape from the yard,
From modern day mysteries to classics by the bard,
Of facts and long numbers, reveal centuries of dates,
A lexical discourse and the wonder it creates.

I read for my future, an escape from these bars,
Of interests and hobbies, sports, fitness and cars,
To learn and develop, to move on from their mire,
A post-prison life worth living and to that I aspire.

I read for my sanity, an escape from this stretch,
Autobiographies and journals, and the joy that they fetch,
For all languages are catered and all religious creeds,
Access for everyone whatever their needs.

I read for the pleasure, an escape from this place,
Literary moments to savour that we all should embrace.
The library packed full of titles, their spines standing on show,
A book is your oyster, so where will you go?

Emotional Endurance

Scarlett Roberts

As my release date draws ever closer, I find myself calmly floating in an entirely nonchalant state between pleasure and oblivion.

I will have been in prison for 129 days.

The record for the longest time of one human being handcuffed to another – and we can safely eliminate any kink relating to the alloy associating them – was 123 days; achieved by a couple who kept breaking up and wanted to save their relationship.

After 123 days they swore never to get back together.

This is how I feel about prison. Or at least it should be, had incarceration not left me emotionally sterile.

Today we were locked in all day due to the inexorable 'staff shortages.' Six staff had accompanied a diabolos double-act to hospital in the night. They had both slit their own throats, leaving Eastwood Park man-down the following day.

'Criminals are the purest of capitalists,' I found myself thinking. 'Anything to get themselves out of the nick for the night.'

The fact that they had to disembowel themselves to derive a divestment to a hospital simply left me feeling rather how Hamlet must have felt about Denmark – a prison he wanted to escape.

One resourceful rapscallion managed to set her own cell alight, complete with her carcass safely enclosed within it. I laughed when I walked past the burnt-out cell. It wouldn't surprise me at all if my eyelids have mutated into nictitating membranes – the laterally operating shutter-like sheaths that reptiles possess instead of eyelids. Reptiles, like me, don't blink when faced with human immolation.

I have not thought about the man I am in love with once. Partly because he's in the US, and instead of accepting that a prison sentence is grounds for separation, I have wholly embraced blaming America and its reproductive rights violations imposed on women: thinly veiled as 'pro-life' in a country where mass shootings and the death penalty are as commonplace as Starbucks Coffee.

I have barely contemplated my monstrously small and overdressed dachshund, Max. I just can't. He's too cute and I'm too imprisoned.

Emotions and immurement are immiscible in order to survive.

I have eight more days and I truly hope my endocrinal lobotomy is reversible

Prison Thoughts
B Child

Why do I have to put up with constant interruptions, frustrations, failure to deliver, the inefficiencies of others? If I do so without complaining, does this make me an idiot, martyr or a saint? Should I protest, stand up and be counted, or am I being British, stoic, a mug? What is it to have such problems and the time to think about them? How on earth can I endure having to contend and resolve this dilemma and still remain sane?

I used to believe that tolerance, endurance, forbearance were all desirable attributes to be encouraged in my family and practiced in my own life. I put up with my wife's idiosyncrasies, she put up with my selfishness, and we both ensured a combined lack of wealth. That was before life changed for us all, and now I have to endure an hour walking round a freezing Brixton yard, surrounded by 20-foot high walls, listening to the views of my companion for the day. My wife has to endure life without me, though she may consider life without me a blessing. Unfortunately, there's no avoiding my condition or my companion of the moment. We have to endure the situation we are in, as others endure theirs. Confinement can be both physical and mental. Behind the Brixton walls, it is clear that the confinement is physical but, only if you allow it, is it mental as well.

So, in my companion's opinion, being a tolerant person was just putting up with things as they were. Nothing to be proud of. Clearly, I couldn't argue; I was used to just accepting things as they were, content to accept anyone else's view. That's why I did it every day; in fact I'd been brought up to do it, so had made a virtue out of it. However, if I have no choice in the matter, no free will, how could this really be saintly or admirable. I don't really choose to endure, I just do. For many people like me, it is the natural state of existence. But he is determined not to let me off the hook that easy and rams his point home. Endurance, he says, is a negative, even self-destructive trait, one that should be challenged. It seems that my companion is right. He has to be.

However, I am not totally convinced, not yet willing to give up a mode of behaviour that has defined my life. Perhaps it's not the fact that people endure but the manner in which they do that's important.

A tenet of many faiths is that it's the human condition to suffer and to endure suffering without complaint. Whether it's an individual accepting the suffering on behalf of the whole of humanity, a community choosing to suffer poverty, periodic fasting and deprivation, or the acceptance that living itself implies suffering. That's hardly a situation that encourages any form of positivity for me.

As I sat by my daughter's bedside all those years ago, I was not too sure that I ever really considered her situation. She endured the suffering imposed on her by another, a situation not of her doing but one that changed her life forever. Yet she endured with a fortitude that all around her could only admire. Certainly, she had been a victim, but her endurance was not one of martyrdom. As I write these words, it's likely that she's enduring now. She had overcome pain and became a new person, gained respect because of how she endured. Her endurance inspired the family to consider others more than they had before. Raising money for the hospital, running a marathon, pushing her in a wheelchair – not so much a feat of endurance as an endurance of the feet. Almost turning endurance into a pleasure. Now, because of my selfish behaviour, my absence has challenged her to endure more suffering. That thought leads me to endure another period of guilt, so here we go again. But has her experience enabled her not just to endure this new situation but instead make it a success? Has her previous conquest completely overcome the idea of endurance for her? Does the very act of endurance remove the concept of suffering?

It may be that the endurance of a prison sentence is more akin to taking part in the Le Mans 24-hour race than spending a long period of time in a hospital. It is a chance to test oneself against time and an unthinking, inanimate body: in one case a race track, the other the prison system. The ultimate Le Mans goal is to produce a faster, more reliable car, better able to cope with the race. For the prisoner, the challenge is: you either endure or you fall apart, run out of fuel, crash and burn, be destroyed by the race itself.

At this moment I am not sure where all this introspection leaves me. Nothing has changed, I am still here, gazing at my own metaphorical navel and enduring the situation that society has condemned me to. Certainly, I could just continue to sit here, but my companion's comments and my daughter's actions suggest that I am allowing myself to be a victim, become a martyr, though I'm certainly not a saint. I'm achieving nothing, not even enjoying revelling in my own inadequacy. If nothing else, I am letting myself down, missing an opportunity by accepting things as they are and enduring them.

Challenging myself to write in response to some random competition, when I had no real thought on the matter, has resulted in a situation that is completely unsatisfactory. Endurance isn't something to be admired. It is to be pitied, challenged, anything but accepted. Instead of just sitting here, wallowing in things as they are, I should do something. I may not be able to change where I am or the people I am with, but I can change the person I am.

Don't endure – empower!

Candy

Daniel Haisley

She would say her name was Candy,
but in fact it was Chariss.
And ever since she was a child,
never had a moment's peace.
Her mother was a timid lady.
Her father was a drunk.
And when she was like 10 years old,
to new depths he had sunk.
He would come and pick Chariss up,
sit her on his knee,
and fondle her innocent body
when nobody could see.
Chariss kept his dirty secret.
She felt all by herself.
It absolutely broke her spirit
And destroyed her mental health.
When Chariss was about 16
and found out her dad was dead,
She went and told her mum what had happened,
but she didn't believe what she said.
Once again Chariss was crushed
and felt all alone,
so packed up the little she had

and ran away from home.
She ran and ran, then ran some more
until she found a spot on the streets,
where she sat and cried her eyes out
while eating a bag of sweets,
Until this guy in a hood came by
and asked Chariss what's wrong.
But when she told him, all he said
was 'Wipe your eyes, you must be strong.
Chariss is dead, you're now called Candy
and with me you're gonna hang.
That family you had is in the past,
your new one is my gang.'
Now at first, everything was great,
Candy would pull her weight.
She helped the gang sell their drugs
To put food on her plate.
But after a few months of this
nothing she did was enough.
She started having sex with them,
She was desperate for their love.
But then one night at a party,
the most brutal thing was done,
They got Candy alone in a room,
And raped her one by one.
So what was left for Candy to do
but run away from them,

turn her heart to solid stone
and never trust again.
She would now go from place to place
off the beaten track.
She started smoking crack cocaine
and then injecting smack.
She would leave her number in phone boxes
advertising sex
and sit eagerly waiting
for a stranger's text.
When she would receive one,
She'd meet them down an alley.
Most of them treated her like scum,
although some of them were pally.
But after many years on drugs,
she couldn't even sell this,
so she took a knife out from her bag
and sliced open her wrists.
She stood there for a brief moment
then fell down with a thud,
and that was the end for poor Candy.
She died in a pool of blood.
So the next time you see an addict
or a homeless and look down your nose,
understand that very rarely
it is a life they've chose.
Some of us are handed wins.

Some of us handed defeats.
And some start out like little Candy
eating a bag of sweets.

Sunday

G Arm

Dawn broken tests and squawked tannoy noise
Wrests, from their stumbler, the scrub-a-dub boys.
No bare torsos, no sliders on the landing.
Sir, boss, or miss to the officers standing.
Dictate demands that association commences.
A 50-minute hour amidst drone-proofed fences.
Timidly, we emerge through punishing warm.
Trading muesli and milk in a bravado swarm.
Secrets. Stretched. Lasting into days, they
Crack, skid and sweat due to laundry delays.
Confidentially queuing for monitored meds.
Stories debunked, beyond, unforgiving beds.
Roll-call stores for ever absent sheets.
Uncared, unheard, over compensating beats.
Deciphering the world via too oft-copied apps.
Laughing out responses on anti-clockwise laps.
Eyes rising, spying, cell-made window-blinds
Hiding the faces of fellow frightened minds.
Promenade punctured by peels of 'Last showers',
Provoking Pavlovian parades back to C wing towers.
Veer by vape beggars to the block saloon doors
Rooting, tooting banter on hair-strewn floors.
Dodge door lock, pad return, soc' soon to cease

Two men, single cell, stainless steel centre piece.
Febrile pharaohs, entombed throughout the day.
As orderlies get fat, we await the sorting hat,
TV on continuous play.

Endurance: Is It Enough?

Bill Franksson

I've been thinking about this for quite a while: endurance. As a serving prisoner, can I get through this part of my life purely as a test of endurance? Winston Churchill is often quoted: 'When you're going through hell, keep going.' This, I think, is the definition of endurance. When all else fails you, rely on your own inner strength to get to the other side, to get to the end, to get to...well, who really knows what tomorrow's dawn will bring.

Tomorrow's dawn, we can take a fairly educated guess at, even in prison. At some point the door will be opened, at some point the door will be shut again. Now consider some others who have faced tests of endurance. Our parents and grandparents may have lived through World War Two, which at times must have seemed like a conflict without end, without certainty, without safety. Or maybe the voyagers seeking the Northwest Passage, locked in ice bound wooden ships. Or, going back to World War Two, the prisoners in concentration camps.

I read a book, *Man's Search for Meaning* by Victor Frankl, an inmate of one of these camps and a psychiatrist. Imagine not knowing with any degree of certainty whether today you would be working the gas chambers or entering them, knowing that your life only has worth to your jailers if you were capable and willing to do what they forced you to do. In that book, which for me was a life lesson and changed the way I am treating this time, one of the questions it poses is: why don't you kill yourself?

Brutal, but those times were brutal, those conditions were brutal. The gist of the first part of the book – I didn't have the wit or will to study and understand the second half – was that, if you haven't ended your suffering through suicide, you must have a reason WHY. That reason is what keeps you going. It may have been fear of death, it may have been a faint hope that you would live through to freedom, it may have been a burning desire to put on record what exactly happened there, it may have been a belief that you would be re-united with loved ones, it may have been a religious belief. It was your personal WHY, your own valid reason. Frankl made the point that, when a person identifies their own personal WHY, then that person can endure any HOW, the HOW being the way that life must be lived, in the case of the camp, with that lack of certainty. Would you live through this day, or the next, or the next?

Even ABBA referenced to endurance,. If you read the lyrics of *The Day Before You Came*, it is such a tedious, daily drag to endure life. It is perhaps one thing after another that is so crushing, but the same thing day after day after day.

Endurance is useful, it enables a person at a basic level to keep going, but it is very much like running into a forest. How far can you run into a forest? Halfway. After that you're running out. Endurance, in prison terms, will only get you to the halfway point at best. To start to run out of the forest, you need to use other tools, which will shrink the size of the forest so that, no matter where you are within your sentence, you are starting to run out of the forest, to an unknown destination at the far edge; in other words, life after release.

The tools for endurance are a WHY, first and foremost, plus

patience, perseverance, the will and the want to endure. This got me through the first year or so of my time inside. But for me it's so unsatisfying. The thought of just 'dour it oot', as it is sometimes said in Ayrshire, was a clue to just how tedious, mind-numbing and time-wasteful endurance was going to be. I didn't want to just endure, I wanted to LIVE. Time to get some more tools.

Each day I start anew, I still don't know with certainty what each new day will bring. I had been watching a tomato plant growing in the weeds outside the cell block. Each day the five tomatoes on the vine got a little plumper. Then one day the gardeners cut it down. I'm pretty sure they just saw a wild-sown plant, an unwanted weed. I was annoyed though, but rather than upset myself for more than a few minutes, I decided to take action. I gathered up the bruised and damaged fruits and wild sowed them on an unused flower bed. They might self-seed, they might just feed the birds. I didn't know the gardeners would cut down what I came to see as my plant, I don't know if it would regrow, but I do know I'll take an interest in its progress. Other tools are memories that I enjoy a ramble through. I also try to complete at least one element of 'just for today.' For example: just for today, I will be happy. Just for today, I will live without fear. (Thank you, AA!)

Being determined to find at least one thing to be grateful for each day, to be open to small flashes of beauty, kindness and compassion and to treat others with respect helps a lot. Endurance alone isn't enough.

We must live as fully as we possibly can!

Dystopia

G. M.

As twilight crept towards the horizon, its ebony claws strangled the sun's golden hues, spilling liquid strands of crimson onto the canvas of the sky, as if foretelling all that was to come.

Darting across the evening sky, swallows chased insects like children running round the school yard. Every airborne turn so sudden and sharp it appeared as if the apex of their angular wings could, at any instant, slice open the heavens. High above, imperious, a red kite circled, observing all below, mimicking the red guard of old Constantinople. Its eyes fixed upon some far distant prey with precise focus and obsessive intent. Its magnificence shimmered in the sun's dying rays.

I looked out from behind the heavily barred window, locked away from Nature's restorative touch. It has been so long since I last saw anyone real, that measurement of time had become an abstract concept. The stench emanating from the adjoining cells was a stark reminder of the predicament I was in. It was not difficult to imagine my neighbours and the decomposing remnants of their bodies bloating in the summer heat. The endless thrum of noise that was so much part of life until recently gradually faded quickly to be replaced by desperate screams and piteous wails. Now even those sounds were only memories; the silence offered absolutely no peace nor solace.

It must have been over a week ago that the staff stopped coming in. The last time I saw any of them, they were dressed in biohazard suits as they threw sealed trays of food through the tiniest gap in the door into our cells. It was much too late for such precautions: someone must have brought the disease in with them and, to my knowledge, no one else left. Our telephones no longer worked, nor was there any power; therefore, access to any information about this latest pandemic was impossible. If others had survived, I didn't know. Maybe immunity existed in others on different wings, but without keys there was no way to know for sure. The only thing that was set in stone was the certainty of my death. I would die cold and alone in this cage and ,every time the sun set, I was one day closer to the inevitable.

The nights dragged on, and the crows argued with such vitriol that, even the dead felt likely to stir from their eternal slumber to voice their complaints. I knew they were trying to force a way through the gaps in the partially opened windows to feast on the glut of positioned carrion that lay in wait for them. The rats, however, were far more adept in their skills and were not frustrated. They clawed their way up the walls and through the network of pipes, fed on corpses and even on the bodies that hadn't quite passed on. The lack of resistance had made them more brazen than ever before. The incapacitated just lay there on their worn mattresses of withered foam. Each cell had become more like a chamber in a morgue than a place for the living.

I was able to cope without food for several weeks, and the plumbing still worked, so I thought there was a faint possibility of survival. What was really killing me was the unknown. My family was hundreds of miles away and they could easily be victims of this plague or, like me, they could have immunity. Hope in prison is a dangerous weapon, often used by the establishment to weaken us, but all I could do was hope with all my heart that my loved ones were safe.

Society had deemed us worthless and, as such, we were not on their list of priorities when it came to the successive waves of pandemics that had plagued the world since the initial outbreak several years ago. The days continued to drift by as I stared out of the barred window, watching the scenery cut apart by the reams of razor wire. The carrion eaters seemed to get closer and closer as I drifted ever closer to my inevitable ending. As I drifted in and out of consciousness, I grasped onto any memory of my beautiful kids, trying to endure so that I might see them again.

Slowly and gradually my breath shortened and I drifted away into nothingness. Forgotten by this system my care had been entrusted to, abandoned by the society that had locked me away. There appeared to be no positive outcome in this situation. Pain coursed through my body, so much so it tore me away from my journey towards the inevitable bright light. Without strength to sit up, I fumbled my way onto the floor. Through half-crusted eyes, I saw the shadows of men trying to move me. The pain that awoke me was from sour smelling bed sores rupturing, leaving tatters of skin attached to the worn mattress and trails of thick yellow fluid dripping from the bed.

Through masks, muffled voices were attempting to communicate, but the voices were so distant and sounded so foreign that they could have been from another planet. The pain that had wrenched me from unconsciousness overcame me and ushered me back into insentience.

When I next opened my eyes all, I saw were burning white lights, round and intense, directly above me. As I began to focus on my new reality, doctors surrounded me. No longer in protective suits, they stood closer than anyone had in the longest time. I had survived the plague and my blood was being harvested to provide antibodies that others needed.

All that mattered to me was my family. I had to endure this dystopian terror so I could return to them.

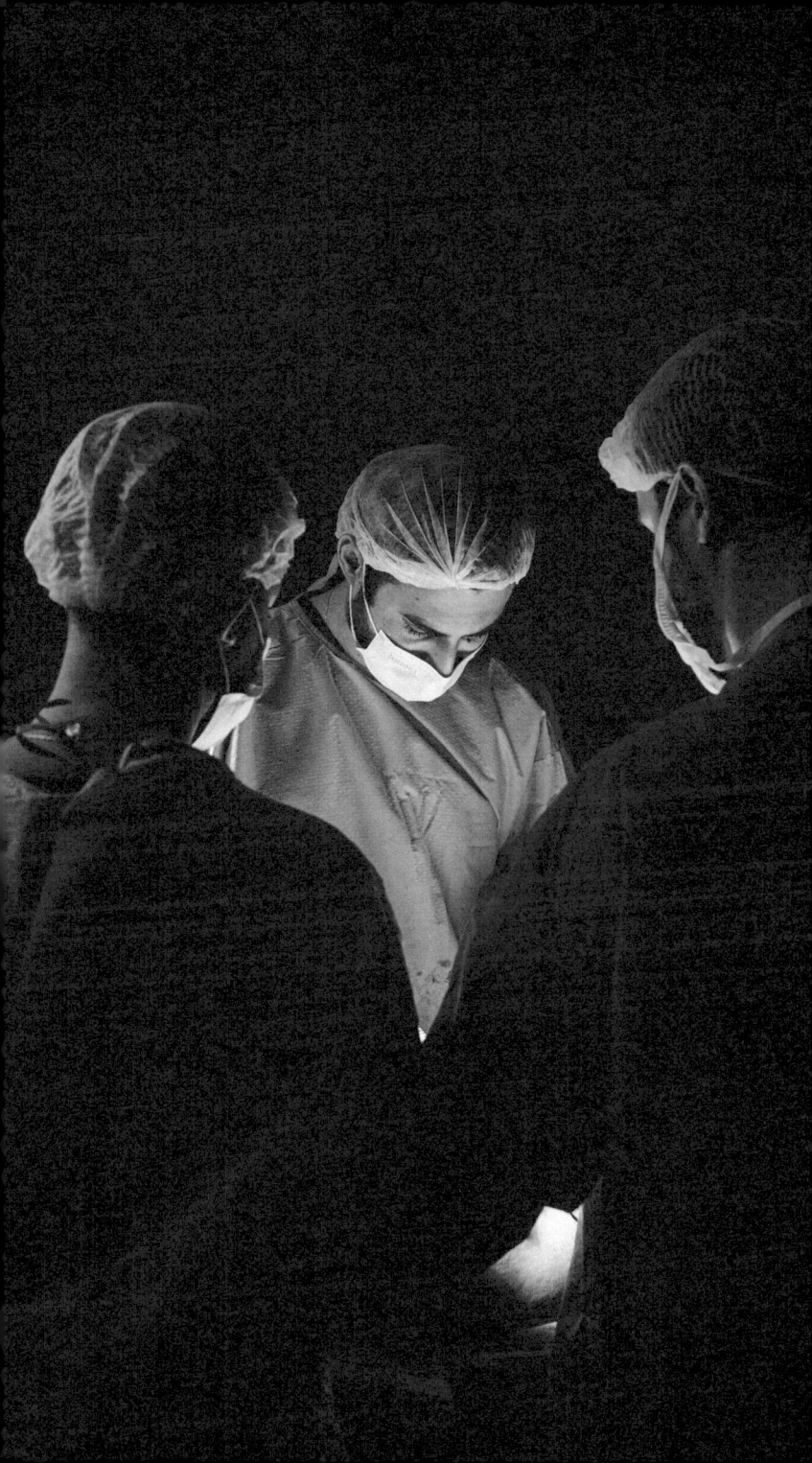

Happy/Unhappy

Jamie H.

I'm doing really well. I'm happy and I'm clean.
I'd go as far as to say it's the happiest I've ever been.
Yes, I might be locked up every single day,
But I'm more happy in every single way.
I've got myself a job, I'm in a good routine,
I'm opened up at 8 o'clock and then I start to get clean.
I sweep and mop the landing,
Then the showers next,
After that I wait downstairs to get my morning meth.
Half past 9 is bang up, I lie back down and read,
Until the door is opened up to let us out to feed.
After I've ate my lunch, I'm banged back up again,
I'm picking up a notepad and I'm looking for a pen.
I'm sweeping up the landing, not long after 2,
But by 3 o'clock I'm finished and there's nothing left to do.
So I go and make a coffee and wait around for food,
Talking shit to people, depending on my mood.
After dinner is soc', but that's a load of shit,
Walking round in circles is about the gist of it.
Finally there comes bang up, the best part of the day,
And when I tell you best, I mean it in every way.
Sitting down to read this, it doesn't sound so great.
All of it in fact, I actually really hate.

I've never been so happy? We both know that's a lie,
It's just a coping mechanism, my way of getting by.

A Disarmed Refrain

Kevin Kane

It was August 1976 – a summer of unwavering sunshine. Nine-year-old Alfie Lemon skipped along the pavement, avoiding the cracks. Five two-pence pieces were entombed within the sweaty confines of his right hand, with no chance of escape.

Alfie had been orphaned as a toddler and was being raised by his grandmother, an austere woman, entrenched in the age of 'children should be seen not heard.' She would cane Alfie for the merest of minor discretions: unfinished Brussel sprouts; a scuffed shoe; a wet bed; a lost button.

The cane's week had been busy testing the young boy's endurance. Earlier that day, Alfie had been sent to tidy 'that pigsty of a bedroom.' Not long after, his grandmother had crept upstairs and caught him listening to his box record-player, a cherished gift from Auntie Ann. 'Alfred Lemon!' she seethed. Five minutes later, Alfie's thighs throbbed. As his grandmother walked out of the room, she muttered to herself, 'Ridiculous song anyway. How can anyone save all their kisses for someone? Whatever next?' Those last two words were a common refrain from Alfie's grandmother. They spat cynicism and, to Alfie, were tightly knotted to the smart of the cane.

Alfie started to run, briefly cooled by the rush of air. Soon, he arrived at his destination. He sat, panting, on the kerb outside the sweetshop, the heat of the pavement immediately evident. He opened his hand and looked down at the copper coins, the green-tinged sweat of his palm glistening in the sun. The money had come from a local pensioner, Mr Tudor, whose bungalow smelled of old chip fat and gas. Mr Tudor would often stand at his door and bark to any passing child while brandishing his walking stick, ordering them to the shop for two ounces of back bacon or a bottle of sterilised milk. There would usually be a few pence left for whichever child had braved the encounter.

Inside the shop, Alfie fidgeted in a queue of eight people, watching the lone shop assistant – a girl in her late teens. She was abrupt and unfriendly with each customer. An elderly couple was standing behind Alfie when he heard the man grumble quietly, 'She's always horrible, this one.'

Alfie stepped up to the counter and tipped his sweaty earnings onto it. 'A KitKat please,' he said. The girl scowled at the coins, sighed then took a KitKat from the adjacent display, placing it onto the counter without a word. Alfie picked it up and went to walk away, but stopped. He turned back to the counter, removed the wrapping from his KitKat, snapped off two fingers and then slid them toward the girl. The girl looked at the chocolate, then eyed Alfie with furrowed puzzlement.

'Don't be sad,' said Alfie.

The girl searched Alfie's face for a few seconds, before her expression softened and her eyes started to fill up. She leaned on the counter, head down, and sobbed without control.

'Well I never!' said the old man behind Alfie. 'What a wonderful young man.' He gently ruffled Alfie's hair. 'Whatever next?'

I Hold the Centre Still

Martin H.

I hold the centre still,
For though my long sleep
Draws ever near
Time has not yet severed
All the threads that
Tie me to this place.
I hold the centre still,
A spider yearning
One last supper
One shining joy before
Winds tear my web and
Like a leaf I fall.
I hold the centre still,
With trembling fingers
I grasp my links
To what little remains
So many links are broken
So many already lost.
I hold the centre still,
The busy world is hushed
As dreams of the past overcome
The urgent calls of the day
I am content, no longer irked

By my oncoming fall.
Strung dewdrop memories blaze
Within the gathering dark
Like dying nova stars.
Inexorably it comes,
My long sleep, but
I hold the centre still.

Reunion

G. M.

Nothing was said on the short taxi ride home; words seemed wrong somehow. To speak would have intruded on the private moments of solace. The couple held hands, but neither could look at the other. Instead they stared vacantly out of the misted window. Such was their distraction that they barely noticed the poor state of the vehicle's upholstery, their attention drawn to a much larger hole in their life.

The cab pulled round the corner and he released his grip on his wife's hand, automatically reached into his pocket and pulled out a crumpled note. He passed the tatty violet piece of paper to the driver as the car came to a halt.

'Keep it.'

The bearded driver was about to protest at such an overpayment, but the couple were already gone. The old man just shrugged his shoulders and turned his well-worn taxi about before driving away into the evening.

It was only just after seven, but the sun had long since fled from the sky and dipped under the horizon. The cold winter air nipped at the skin of any who braved the bitter evening. Trees cast eerie silhouettes as their leafless forms reached into the night sky in a vain attempt to grab the distant stars. An urban fox, scavenging inside the torn remnants of a discarded bin bag was the only other occupant on the snow covered street. It was completely oblivious to the couple walking up their driveway while it scattered debris across the pavement in its search for a tasty morsel or two.

The evening's silence was broken by the metallic grating as he tried to fit the key into the lock. After several efforts, it finally found its way home and, with a series of clicks, the tumblers turned and the bolt released its grip on the frame. Unoiled hinges screeched painfully as the door opened.

The couple stepped inside the cold house that no longer felt like a home. Without looking, she reached for the light switch in the hall, then instinctively typed a four-digit code on the rubberised keypad that disabled the alarm.

Turning to face her husband, she almost fell into his arms as she squeezed herself tightly against him. Searching for comfort, she buried her head into the hollow where his neck met his shoulder. Sobbing uncontrollably, her perfect mask of composure she'd worn all day finally slipped. She could at last release the flood of tears she had held back for so long. Her husband, suffering every bit as much, held her tightly, trying his best to offer what scant comfort he could.

Eventually she pulled away, his collar stained with tears, mascara and makeup but neither he nor his wife cared. The day had already been too long, too painful, to be bothered about such trivial matters. Of greater concern were the deeper and darker stains, blood red blemishes that could never be erased.

The couple stepped into the darkened lounge, a faint orange glow from the streetlights cast strange shadows around the room. Reaching for the amber bottle he poured a very large measure of the bitter spirit before downing it in one.

'Are you sure?' he asked his wife.

'Definitely,' came the reply through despairing sobs.

In unison, they headed up the stairs, each step bringing them closer to their sombre destination. They removed their coats, left them on the floor where they fell. There seemed little point in hanging them up.

She reached into an open drawer in the bedside cabinet and removed several bottles of vividly coloured pills. A rainbow of relief reminded her of all the wonderful childhood treats that had brought so many smiles to her son's adorable face. She emptied out the pills and divided them into approximately even piles before handing one pile to her beloved.

In one hand, he held the bottle of single malt that he had saved for a special occasion. A gift from his son, the last gift his boy had ever bought him. His only child whom he had placed in the ground earlier that day.

With a stream of tears rolling down his cheeks, he tilted his head and poured a handful of the brightly coloured tablets into his mouth. He took a large swig of whisky and swallowed. Twice more he repeated this before passing the bottle to his childhood sweetheart, who followed his lead and did the same. Afterwards, the two lay on their bed and held each other tightly as they drifted off to meet their son.

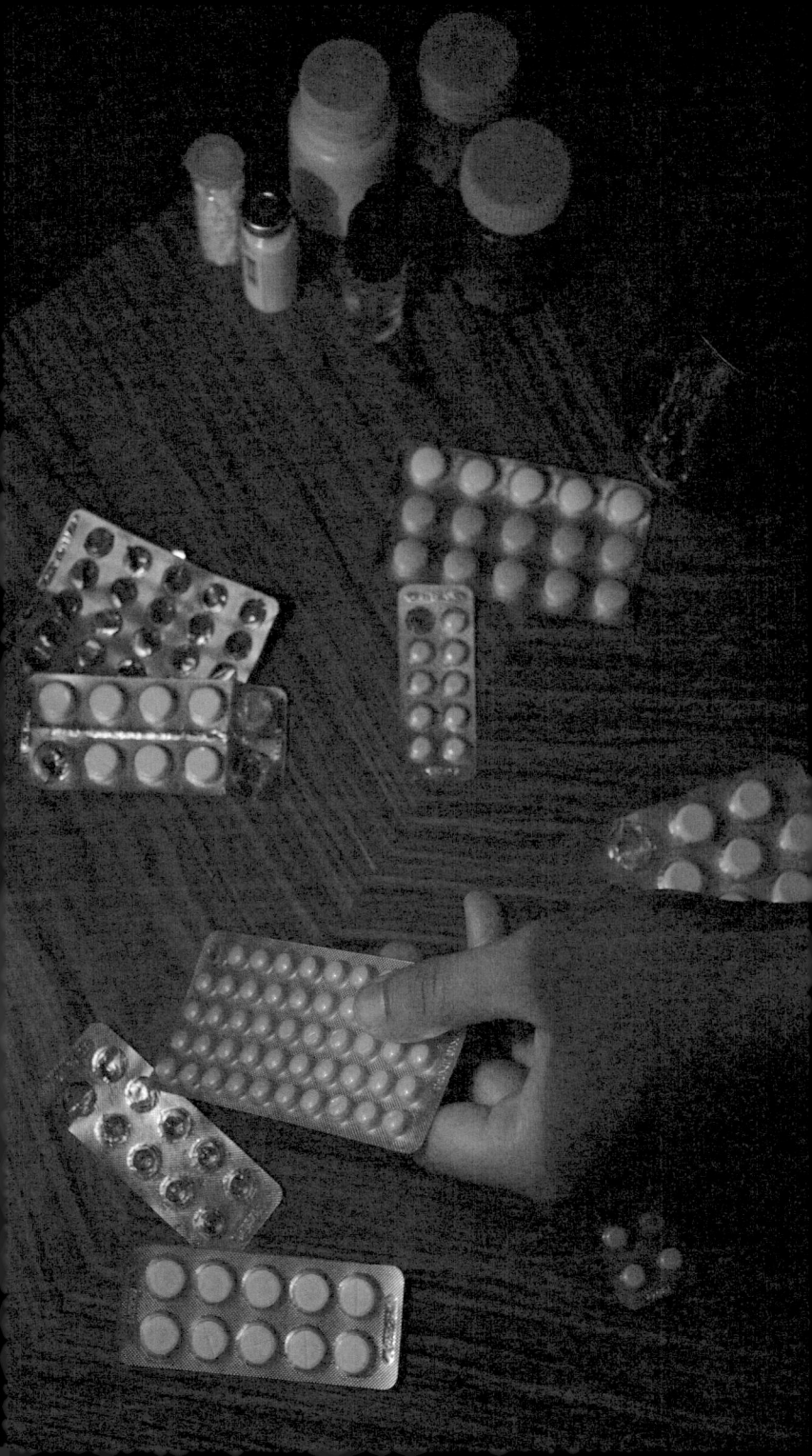

You

Ekimlláh

You keep judging me from the outside.
What about my brain or my heart, the stuff inside?

You keep asking where I really come from.
I say over and over again, I am from London
You give me a cynical smile,
as if to say what a disillusioned and stupid child.

You brought me here,
I didn't just appear!
You sent for me to rebuild and work
On the jibs you didn't like or would rather shirk.

Now the fruit is ripe and ready to be shared,
You want the bigger half; that's weird!

You say take what you get,
It is your best bet.
You are not entitled to any more.
You are beneath us under the floor.

You keep the power and wealth amongst you
And construct the laws so that they favour you.

And when I call you out, you say it is not true.
You say you are not so racist, not like before.
And you don't use the 'P' or 'N' word,
So, I should not be so sore.
You've gone from overt to convert,
So, I should be over the moon
Cause now you are singing a different tune.

You appoint the token to appease the minority
And say you are doing your bit to promote an equal society,
But I see right through the lies and hypocrisy.
This is just to keep me in check and it's not a conspiracy.

50/50, is that not fair?
Your pound of flesh is over there!
Not an ounce more you have to share.

Instead, you would rather I drink from the poisoned chalice
Tell me, why are you so full of malice?

Why do I make you so sick?
Is it because I have a bigger ….?

What have I done to deserve this hurt?
Have I not been here as long as you on this earth?
Despite all that, I don't seek revenge, nor retribution,
I just want to be treated equally and recognised for my contribution.

I can't breathe, get off my back?
We are the same, that is a fact.

Red, green, yellow or blue,
I may look different, but I am human too.
Cut my hand and I will bleed,
Same as you, you have to concede.

If I kneel on your neck you will die.
I am sure you don't want me to give it a try.

So, look in the mirror and tell me what you hear.
Can you hold my inequality stare?
Can you see the smell I have to bear?
Can you understand why I live in fear?
Can't you feel my pain?
You put it there!

OK, what's done is done, what is to be must be.
We must learn from history.
Not just the good stories, but the bad ones as well.
The truth must be told; the truth you must tell.

So, let's rearrange and make positive change,
So that future generations don't see colour so strange.
There is no point quarrelling and fighting with each other.
We are from the same creator.
You are my brother.

Forgiveness is Power

Mr Hughes

Over the years I have heard many speak
about their own sense of guilt and the forgiveness they seek.
They speak about shame and events from the past,
but a time has to come, when forgiveness can last.

Of course, an apology won't vanish the truth,
all the wrong that was done, all the pain and proof.
There must be a point in the journey ahead,
where forgiveness is key to a life well led.

Forgiveness is power, it frees the constraints,
to overcome obstacles and rid former traits.
Each of us hold the keys to forgive,
you must use them wisely, you have a life to be lived.

So before you go and try to move ahead,
you must always remember a saying once said.
We can be our own enemies in trying to move on,
so learn to forgive first, and accept what has been done.

Forgiveness is power, it can work both ways,
in the forgiver and forgiven, in turn it portrays.
It can help with them both, if you allow it to,
but first it must start with the importance of you.

To forgive yourself first will have a ripple effect,
so open your heart, that you have been trying to protect.
Like a stone that is thrown in a pond nearby,
the ripples go outwards, and reach far and wide.

So forgive yourself first, and throw your first stone,
and see how the ripples will reach those at home.
No matter how much you stumble or fall,
forgiveness is key, for yourself, one and all.

When Two Became One

Mr Hughes

Depending on a person's past, or because of difficult and challenging events they may have experienced in life, the understanding and perceptions of the word endurance will ultimately vary from person to person. For me, endurance is simply having the ability to withstand prolonged hardship. Every day, all around us, we are surrounded by people, who have, through no fault of their own, found themselves empowered by endurance. People with disabilities, communities and households faced with poverty, countries dealing with war and conflict, or the aftermath of natural disasters and victims of crime. I have a great deal of admiration and respect for the people who possess the gift of resilience. I admire their ability to find the positives and move on from what can be the darkest of times.

For me, and for many of my fellow prisoners, of which I have met many during my time in prison, we often find ourselves trying to use the skills of resilience and endurance. While we carry out our punishment and try to get used to our surroundings, the majority of us are ultimately trying our utmost to become better people.

For many of us in prison, there is, however, a constant battle with a haunting of our own. Against a demon that has the ability to feed from any thoughts we may have of hope and endurance. That demon comes in the form of forgiveness.

For me, I feel strongly that forgiveness and endurance are both equally as important as each other. However, more importantly,

I believe that for either of them to be effective, they must accept the other by their side. People will have different ideas and understandings about the meaning of forgiveness. I believe that a person forgives when, and if, they choose not to hold on to bitterness and hatred. Instead, they set themselves free from being trapped in the negatives of past events, and let go. This, of course, will be extremely hard for any victim of crime, and one often thinks about whether this should ever be expected. What I can tell you is that, for most of us in prison, we are remorseful and carry our stumbling block around with us every day in the form of guilt and shame. This alone, stops people moving forward in life and prevents the importance of endurance being effective in one's life.

It is important to remember that forgiveness does not mean that wrong actions do not matter, do not hurt or should not be justly punished. From experience, I can tell you that it is happening every day in prisons. It is evident in everyday life, behind the prison walls and behind cell doors. People coming to terms with the poor choices and judgements they have made, and now facing the consequences as a result. But much deeper than that, people are trying to forgive themselves, longing to be forgiven and carrying the constant weight of guilt and shame for what happened in the past. What has happened to them, and their own actions, what their families have been through because of their actions and, of course, the victims of crime.

To grasp endurance and for it to be effective, we must find a way to forgive ourselves first. It must start with ourselves. There has to come a point when we can face our mistakes, learn to forgive our own actions and the hurt we have caused others.

Can endurance really work without first learning to forgive ourselves? This may be a question for all of us in prison, but I believe we can go through our daily regime in here, surrounded by the constant reminders that we are being punished for our actions. But for endurance to be effective, forgiveness is key, and that has to start with ourselves. Without it, will we really have the ability to withstand prolonged hardship? I think not.

A prison sentence is just the start. For most, we will always punish ourselves with the guilt and shame that we will carry with us forever. But if we can learn the power of forgiveness, then endurance will play an active role in helping us to move on and gain the ability to withstand the prolonged hardship in the form of learning to live with our past mistakes. One thing I am sure of, is that we all have the power to forgive and we should use that power wisely.

Eternal Darkness of the Enduring Mind

G. D. Lusty

Anna's eyes opened, slightly at first, as if she had just wakened from a long slumber, but with no change. There was nothing, an unlit nothingness; darkness ensued the sound of silence. Anna reached out with every fibre of her being, but there was still nothing. At first she couldn't tell if she was standing or lying down. Anna tried to stretch her arms out in front of her, but to no avail. Then to her sides; nothing. Finally behind her; still nothing. Anna suddenly felt dizzy as she couldn't even see her arms reaching out, or her body for that matter. She must be standing up, she thought to herself as she felt for the ground.

'What? This can't be!' Anna screamed as if shouting at a light bulb suddenly gone out.

'Hello! Is anyone there?' she asked, then listened for a reply.

But there was no answer, not even an echo, not even the sound of silence. There was no sound at all. Anna could hear herself in her head but wasn't sure if that sound had come out of her.

She felt for her body, then her mouth. 'Thank god, I'm here. I'm naked, but I'm here', she thought to herself. But the joy of feeling her body slowly faded as she realised she didn't know where 'here' actually was.

'Help! Help! My name's Anna and I'm stuck in here.' Anna paused and listened again.

Silence, again.

'Why am I here? What did I do? Who put me here? Where is here? Why have I no clothes? Where are my clothes? Why can't I see? Why is it dark? Where are the walls? Where is the floor? Ooh, I don't want to be here no more.'

Anna sobbed into herself. She felt the tears build up in her eyes, but they didn't go anywhere. Her tears just formed into a larger puddle until she wiped them away with her hand. Only a few minutes passed, but to Anna this felt like hours.

'Am I dead? Is this what death is like? Am I in hell because this is certainly not heaven? Ooh, how would I know what heaven is like, it's not like I've been there, I don't even believe in god for goodness sake.'

Anna thought about her life, every action, every decision and interaction she had ever made, then she began to imagine a door opening in front of her and light shining in on her, illuminating her way out of this place.

'When I get home, I won't take people for granted. I promise I won't. I will enjoy every second, every moment, even that annoying sound my boyfriend makes when he's chewing his food. Ooh how I would give anything to hear Ben's voice right now, telling me to calm down and that this is all a dream.'

'Wait a minute. Ben!'

Anna realised that she hadn't given a single thought to where she had been before this darkness.

Anna opened her eyes and looked over at Ben sitting in the corner of the room, slouched over and drawing back the heroin into his needle from a dirty spoon. Then she looked at her own arm, the needle was still hanging out of her vein but the heroin was long gone.

'Ben, make me another hit up again please, babe.'

Endurance is Meaningless?

Thomas Brian Finn

The circle never closes
The square is set in stone
It's never beds of roses
But a lifetime to atone—

First primal breath of air
Begins fleeting loss and gain
Temporary triumphs, pains forebear
No quick finish; false starts in vain—

The life of an amoeba
A solitary drive
To meaningless existence
So good to be alive—

Could it be possible
Or the death of a dream
Those hedonistic flights,
The cat's got the cream—

Race to the finish friend
A marathon, sprint, or mile
Struggles in the straights or bend
First or last; doing is worthwhile—

It's over in just a second
Those thousand years of pain
Another chance to pay the bond?
There is no such path again.

Endurance

John C.

As the moon doffed its hat in deference to the sun, glints of sunlight announced the arrival of dawn and welcomed in the beginnings of a new day. For Herbert Riley, however, it was going to be just another day to be endured rather than enjoyed. Subsisting solely on a basic state pension and forced to choose between heating or food, the prospect of yet another December day held little appeal. Living alone with only his little dog Archie for company, the icy cold of December hung in the air as dense and brittle as a lump of hard toffee. With no heating, Herbert sat in his front room huddled under a blanket.

It had been like this for weeks. His frail body, sustained only by a cheap, limited diet, shivered uncontrollably, causing every pre-Christmas day to be a battle of endurance. And the loneliness was just as depressing and soul destroying.

With two sons living locally, he hoped they would call in to see him occasionally. But, with families of their own, they were always, it seemed, too busy. Hearing a carol being played on the radio, he envied those who could enjoy a family Christmas. Suddenly the gnawing pain in his heart caused his eyes to well up and, seconds later, he felt the tears dribbling down his cheeks. Sensing his master's distress, Archie licked Herbert's hand. Herbert stroked his only friend's head, grateful for this little bit of love.

A minute or so later, and more in hope than expectation, Herbert reached for his newspaper to check his lottery number against the result.

He studied the ticket number. Then he looked at the winning number on the page. They matched. Herbert swallowed hard and checked again. In disbelief, he checked several times more. The result was the same: he had won. He checked the rollover prize value: £81.5 million. He stared at the paper in shock. He switched on the fire and central heating. He phoned the lottery company who confirmed his win. He then rang the bank. He asked for £1,000 loan until the check cleared. Anxious to retain his account, the manager knocked his door an hour later holding the cash and a box of fancy cakes. Herbert, for the first time in months, smiled and felt his heart lighten. He thanked the manager, looked him in the eye. Herbert had a plan.

'Let's go, shall we?' the old chap asked.

The smile on the manager's face flickered. 'Go where?' he asked, puzzled.

'To the supermarket,' Herbert replied, happily.

Hardly in a position to refuse, the manager agreed, his tone feigning an enthusiasm he didn't feel.

Herbert thought back to the loneliness, cold and shortage of food he'd endured for so long, and felt determined to enjoy a different and happy Christmas as he had when he was younger.

Sitting in the back of the man's Rover, he reflected upon his former despondency and was struck by the moral of his story. Dark clouds and a silver lining loomed large, as did a lesson taught to him by his endurance: that which doesn't t kill you, you emerge from stronger. A lesson for us all, he reflected, a lesson for us all.

A Little Longer…
J.P. Wooton

Sarah considered herself a strong person, able to endure anything. The things she'd faced in life – her parents splitting when she was nine, the destruction of their family home, even the tragic loss of her younger sister – had taken their toll, of course, but she'd got through it. This however, was different; she'd never felt pain like it.

Since she was a young teenager, Sarah dreamed about being a mum. She was practical about it: it would happen when she was on her feet financially and in a loving relationship. She would give her child – boy or girl, she had no preference – the best start in life and one filled with happiness. She'd envisaged living in the suburbs: a nice front lawn, a backyard for play and a house stuffed with toys.

Now she had the home and the man. For over six years, she'd been madly in love with Gerard. They were OK moneywise. Not wealthy, but they had enough to cover the mortgage and other essentials, with a bit left over to put away for the baby when it came. If it came. They'd been trying for 18 months with no luck. Sarah tried everything from monitoring her ovulation periods to fortifying Gerard's food with zinc. But nothing worked.

A few months earlier, Sarah was overcome with a feeling that finally, after all this time, she was pregnant. She couldn't explain it. There were no physical signs, just a feeling: pure instinct. It was so strong she fought back the tears threatening to pour from her out of sheer joy. She cut a shopping trip short, unable to ignore the need to get home and take a test.

The house was empty. Gerard was working late again. She dropped the shopping bags at the door and rushed upstairs. She completed a pregnancy test and waited the prescribed two minutes. They felt an eternity. Seconds ticked and her certainty waned. The memory of all the negative results surfaced. She was frightened. The last of her hope drained away. It was going to be negative. She glanced at the panel. PREGNANT. She couldn't believe her eyes, she couldn't react. The tears came. She was overwhelmed with joy. Her dreams were coming true. After all the hurt, the depression, the anxiety, she had finally done it. In her excitement, she couldn't wait until Gerard got home. She bounced up and down, waiting on him to pick up his phone. Finally, he answered.

'Hi honey, what's going on?'

She began to ramble, saying everything at once and not making sense.

'Sarah, slow down. I can't make you out.'

'Gerard, I'm pregnant, you're going to be a dad. You're going to be a dad!'

Gerard was speechless. He too wanted this so much. Perhaps not as much as Sarah but he was overjoyed.

'Fucking yes!' he shouted with his usual delicacy. 'I'm on the way to the car. I'll be home soon.'

Gerard switched the phone to Bluetooth and turned on the ignition. Sarah launched into another 100-mile-an-hour pronouncement, not stopping to draw breath, 'If it's a boy we'll call him Ciaran after my dad we'll get him one of them wee Nike tracksuits for babies and he'll look so cute. If it's a girl: Melissa. I've always loved the name she could wear the wee tracksuit too.'

Gerard chuckled. They'd had this conversation a hundred times, every night for months, as they lay in bed, this was all they talked about. Well, all Sarah talked about. Her face lit up each time. But, as negative tests started to build up, those discussions faded. Sarah's light faded. Bedtime was quiet and she'd slipped into a deep depression. Eventually, sex became less passionate, more routine and mechanical. That didn't matter now. They'd done it.

***

They booked a doctor's appointment the next morning. Sarah was vibrating with excitement, and then she was poked and prodded and, back in the reception area, she waited for news of her baby.

Gerard looked up as the nurse beckoned them. She didn't look pleased. His heart sank, bad news. Sarah seemed blissfully unaware. He hoped he was wrong.

'I'm afraid I've bad news. I'm sorry, Sarah, but you're not pregnant,' the doctor said.

Sarah and Gerard's world crumbled. Sarah heard nothing after those words. Gerard retained enough composure to continue.

'But the pregnancy test?'

'Yes, unfortunately, home tests can be unreliable. They often produce false positives. And even false negatives. My advice? Keep trying. There's no reason you shouldn't be able to conceive. It will happen eventually.'

***

The next few months were terrible. Gerard went to work, returning each evening to find Sarah prostrate on the sofa, TV on, staring into nothingness, her eyes puffy from crying. Each night in bed, she lay in silence, still in the same trance until she drifted off. One day she seemed to come round and declared she wanted to try again. Gerard happily obliged, hopeful that this was a return to normality. Unfortunately, it lasted only a few days. Sarah fell back into despondency.

Thus, one night, Gerard returned home to find Sarah lying on the sofa. He looked down at her and was suddenly filled with an intense love for her. He whispered her name and gently shook her. 'Time for bed, love.' But she didn't respond. He tried again. And again. And again.

***

His lawyer, Rory, explained the inquest process to Gerard. It was straightforward. The coroner would receive the medical reports and formally declare Sarah had died by suicide, a drugs overdose, resulting from depression about her inability to conceive.

Gerard was surprised when he looked at his phone and saw five missed calls from Rory. He called him immediately.

'Hello?'

'Good afternoon, Gerard. How are you?'

'I'm OK, thanks. Is something wrong?'

Rory cleared his throat before continuing.

'I received a copy of Sarah's pathology report. I'm afraid there's no gentle way of putting this. When Sarah died… she was pregnant.'

It was the only time…
that time stood still

Paul J.M.

I was forever drowning on dry land
until one winter's night
a search for sobriety
through frozen fields of snow
all roadways abandoned behind me
and my shadow ominous
moving to the singular sound
of my footsteps breaking new ground
as snowflakes thawed on cold skin
a walk beyond consequence
the soft moonlight and survival
absorbed in the silence
until another sound
shattered the dream—

Crouching, I scanned for clarity
an animal? Cattle?
a slow trudging
my imagination scrutinised the icy light
then, less than two feet away
a beautiful black horse

his nostrils flaring
smoke from his breath—

I placed a hand on his forehead
rubbed his neck
he spluttered approvingly
with acceptance and peace
my heart beat audible
eyes scared and sober
until I too surrender
the trauma, the hurt, the grief
for this moment in time
this moment in time—timeless.

Untitled

Jen McPherson

It was late August. The heady summer days stretched out before me longer than the sun's rays. The days, weeks and months before I arrived had been a whirlwind of chaotic madness which had culminated in my arrest.

I looked out the tiny window of the police van that brought me here and wondered what this place would be like. I was terrified.

This was prison.

I took a deep breath and stepped out of the van onto the jet-black tarmac. In every direction, there was a high fence reminding me that I was now like a wild animal, trapped within a cage.

The first few days were a blur. My behaviour was erratic. I was taken to the mental health wing because I was still psychotic and unwell.

It is hard to describe how claustrophobic a prison cell is. It is just you, your thoughts and those grimy four walls. It allows you to do a lot of thinking, which is not helpful when you are suffering from psychosis.

I couldn't turn on the television in my cell because I thought the newsreaders were speaking to me. I was conscious that I was being filmed inside and outside of my cell. I couldn't eat the food because I was convinced someone was poisoning me.

My mood was low. All I could think about was my elderly father. What kind of daughter was I? I felt suicidal. I soon got hold of a razor and carved deep cuts in my arms. Seeing the blood ooze was a release of my psychic pain.

I made friends with another prisoner called Ellie. She was covered in bruises. She was frail and reminded me of a sparrow. She kept saying to me, 'Why am I here?' We sat in the garden which one of the prison officers had planted and drank cups of tea in the late summer sun. Our moment of peace was soon interrupted by a prison officer bellowing, 'Lock-up!' We said goodbye and rushed to our prison cells.

I soon realised that the way to get out of your cell, and away from your thoughts, was to get a job. I applied for a job in the prison library. This would prove to be my salvation. The library was an escape from prison life. It was as though you were out in the real world again. Prisoners would come in for the latest crime series, biography or romantic fiction. The most popular books, however, were the prison diaries. It was a privilege being able to hand out books to these prisoners.

Each book I read while locked up in my prison cell healed me by some small measure. I was soothed about my mother's death by reading Wild by Cheryl Strayed. I was prepared for my life in a psychiatric ward by reading The Shock of the Fall by Nathan Filer. I was reminded of my university days by reading The Secret History by Donna Tartt. McEwan, Tremain, Ishiguro – they all came to my rescue in my time of need.

However, it was one book t saved my life, Man's Search for Meaning by Viktor E Frankl. I read it and re-read it, underlining passages in a frenzy. My favourite line was, 'He who has a why to live for can bear with almost any how.' My 'why' was my father. I knew I had to continue to live for his sake.

My delusions were getting worse. I thought there was a parasite in my brain slowly killing me. 'Please help me, I will soon be dead,' I would plead to the prison officers.

Thankfully, I soon saw a psychiatrist in the prison. She put me on anti-psychotic medication, which partially helped ease my delusions. I told her about my revelation in Man's Search for Meaning. She noted that I had lost weight because I wasn't eating.

I soon got used to the rhythm of prison life. Every time my father visited me, I would cry afterward. When I was in my prison cell, I would listen to classical music concerts on Radio 3 and weep at how beautiful the music was juxtaposed with my grim surroundings.

I felt completely worthless. It didn't matter how many times I showered in prison, I still felt dirty. Prison exacerbated my mental illness, which was later to be diagnosed as bipolar disorder. Being locked in a prison cell for most of the day was not conducive to recovery from such a serious illness. It managed the illness, rather than treating it.

The kindness of one prison officer stopped me self-harming. When he was on shift, my mood would lift. He would talk for hours with me, encouraging me to think about my future outside of prison. His compassion was a balm to my wounds. I will never forget him.

The other prisoners on the mental health wing soon became my family. Their stories were heart-breaking. There was Sonia, who had killed her baby then tried to kill herself but survived. There were Clara and Emily who hanged themselves on the main wing of the prison but were luckily caught in time. There was Paula who liked being in prison because she had no friends or family on the outside so kept reoffending. Desperation amplified.

When I finally went to court, six months after being on remand in prison, I was sentenced to a hospital order in a low secure unit.

I told Ellie I would write to her. We hugged. I gave her some lavender scented body cream as a parting gift. Would I ever see her again? Probably not. What is true though is that all these women would hold a special place in my heart forever.

What did I learn from my time in prison? Prison taught me to endure darkness, it taught me to survive my illness, but most of all it taught me to cherish the light.

The light remains.

Angels & Demons

Piaras Heatley

Massive Attack, *Paradise Circus*...I tried to kill myself to this song. I nearly succeeded. I still deal with the consequences eight years later. I will always remember the decision being made. I still don't fully understand why I did this. I wanted to live a life I thought I couldn't and still haven't experienced...

I hear keys rattling. My heart races faster. The pain in my back ceases to be. My fingers close to fists, my legs become whips, my mind focuses on looking dangerous, and I begin to...... How many will I have to fight... Don't let them pass the door... Keep them in the narrow of the cell... force them to fight me one at a time...... The training kicks in.....

....How many times have I been on the other side of a door waiting to attack... or anticipating to defend....

....I have to remind myself: 'YOU ARE NOT IN DANGER' 'NO ONE IS COMING FOR YOU' 'AND YOU ARE NOT AFTER ANYONE'....

....The pain in my back slowly fades to it's constant, consistent irritation... Just like the rest of me it won't give up... I refused to die that day.....

.....My mother said I was the colour of my bluest jacket... She probably thought she'd lost her son... The doctor said,

'You might never walk again'..... yet HERE I STAND!!! WALK!!!..... and run away.........but come back to FIGHT!!!...

......Here I crawl to a probably early grave...

I'm so happy that I'm sad that I've sinned, and with all her sense, she loved me though I cheated, lied, and broke her heart.....

......I have dreams of the glint of a knife reflecting streetlights.....Niall calls my name and I turn, and the blood is everywhere, and I can't breathe and wake up screaming and.....

.....Those doctors told me I had kidney failure due to rhabdomyolysis. They said I was lucky to be alive, not brain dead, and might not be able to walk properly again.......

......'No, lads, I'll give the bar a miss'...... 'No! I can't'... 'People will stare at my leg'.. 'I shouldn't be drinking anyway'.....

........I'm probably one of the strongest, fittest people in this prison with severe nerve damage, chronic back pain, probably sciatica and manic depression with PTSD symptoms....

.....Niall died two years later at a house party.... The knife went through his neck. I was in Glasgow with the girl I only realised I cared so much about after I broke her heart, and came to prison for five years......

.......My father told me he had cancer over a prison phone.....

.....You could hear the machines that kept him breathing.....

.......He told me he loved me and was sorry......

...I still have dreams that he's alive....

WHAT THE FUCK AM I?!?.... I don't feel anything..... I mimic emotion.... I AM NUMB!!...numb...

....Now I soak the page with tears.....

All my friends, dead....

.....My family, broken......

....The girl I love probably forgets the silly games we played.....

I love my family. I want to make them proud..... I feel everything again. Emotion floods my heart in a sweeping motion and I decide that I'm happy today....

.....No one answered their phone.....

....All my friends are dead.... Why am I still alive? How did I survive? Why did I not die when....

.....Knife went through my palm....

...He only took one pill and died.....

.....that Dublin one left me for dead.....

......at one stage I probably would have done the same....

....Conan was only out of jail.....

Maria's two sons both dead..... Ronan thanked my mum & sister at the funeral.....

There has to be some fucking reason I'm still alive……

I have to help somehow….
 ……I have to make things right….
 ….I have to keep on going…..

…..but I can't do this anymore…..
 ….Don't say those things to me!….
 ….why am I still alive…..

….They said I should be dead….

I'll always remember the decision being made. I have to help someone with the life I have who cheated death on three occasions. I need to let people know it's 'ok not to be ok'… reputation being everything – the man I once was – rather than being honest with myself I decided to die. In this underworld we live in, we think ourselves strong, we think ourselves invincible. Let me tell you, the money, the drugs, the power, the hate and anger that all comes with it……

…..it makes you more isolated, more vulnerable…… a pocket full of money has no room to hold a hand….. a mind full of anger has no room to be at peace….

….You need to understand yourself to love yourself….

And you need to love yourself to have any type of happy life.....

.....Don't you just want to be happy?

If I can endure these hardships, and I show only glimpses of many....

......Then so can you!....
Don't give up....

.....No matter what you do....

.....Never give up.....
Now I know.... In order for me to be happy, I need to help at least one person realise that there's more to life than drugs, money and power.....

.....Your power is inside your mind.....
There is happiness in finding the will to better ways.

I've days where I lose my willpower, and still battle my demons. Sometimes the demons win. Sometimes the demons nearly wipe me off the board. Sometimes the demons check my king and I've to sacrifice part of myself....

.....But I never, ever give up!..... I'll win the war within myself by not participating as the aggressor....

.....I'll hold my demons' hand, and listen to them, and find out what's really wrong....

......I begin to understand myself.....

.....I know now.....
I'm my demons just as I'm my angels.....